Stegosaurus

Chinese woman

Benz car

king

caveman

Find the answers at the back of the book.

Roman

longboat

settler

saddle

papoose

knight

Diplodocus

First published in Great Britain 1978 by Purnell Books.
Copyright © 1978 Grisewood & Dempsey Ltd.
This edition is published by Derrydale Books, a division
of Crown Publishers, Inc.

Library of Congress Cataloging in Publication Data

Manley, Deborah.
  It's fun finding out about long ago.

  (It's fun finding out about)
  SUMMARY: Text and pictures present a brief and easy-
to-understand view of people and life in the past.
  1. History—Juvenile literature. [1. World
history. 2. Civilization—History] I. Maclean, Moira.
II. Maclean, Colin. III. Gregory, Sally. IV. Title.
D21.1.M36 1979 909 79–54243
ISBN 0–517–30343–4

a b c d e f g h

Printed and Bound in Hong Kong
by Leefung-Asco Printers Limited

It's Fun Finding Out about Long Ago

Words by
Deborah Manley

Pictures by
Moira and Colin Maclean
Kailer-Lowndes
and
Sally Gregory

DERRYDALE BOOKS

Contents

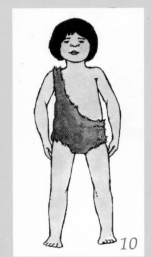

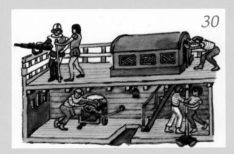

Food from long ago

Machines long ago

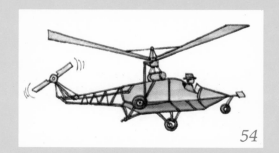

The story of flight

How people lived
in palaces

About children

An old house
in town

The American Indians

The story of transport

How a village grew

Settlers and pioneers

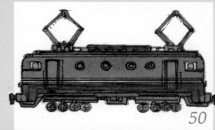

Early trains

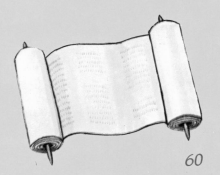

It's fun
finding out

The days of the cowboys

Along the roads

The world of dinosaurs

Long, long ago, long before people lived
on Earth, great reptiles called dinosaurs lived here.
You can see from the picture how huge they were.

Stegosaurus had a spiny
back to protect itself.

Diplodocus was
the longest land
animal that
ever lived.

Some dinosaurs
were quite small.

Tyrannosaurus
ate smaller
dinosaurs.

The size of present-day creatures

giraffe

horse

man

6 feet
(2 meters)

8 feet
(2.5 meters)

19 feet
(6 meters)

Pteranodon had wings made of skin.
It could glide in the air.

Plesiosaurus lived
in the sea and
hunted fish.

When this Tyrannosaurus
died it fell into
the mud.

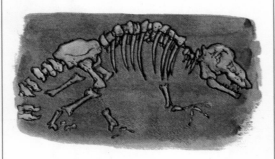

After a long time mud
and stone covered its
bones. The bones
turned into fossils.

People found the fossils.
They rebuilt the
Tyrannosaurus.

They put it into
a museum. People
go and look at it.

People who lived in caves

Long, long ago people lived in caves.
They hunted wild animals. They made
clothes from the animal skins. They
cooked and ate the meat of the animals.

They made boats from logs.

How a caveman made tools

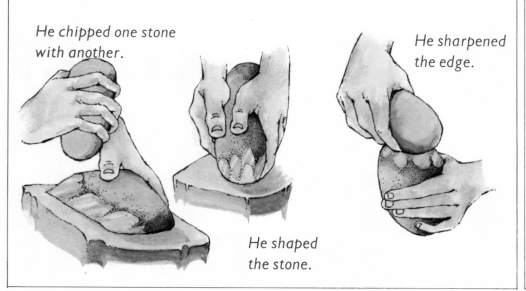

He chipped one stone with another.

He shaped the stone.

He sharpened the edge.

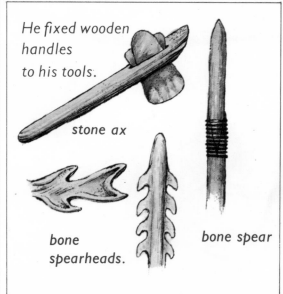

He fixed wooden handles to his tools.

stone ax

bone spearheads.

bone spear

Some cave people painted pictures on the walls of their caves.

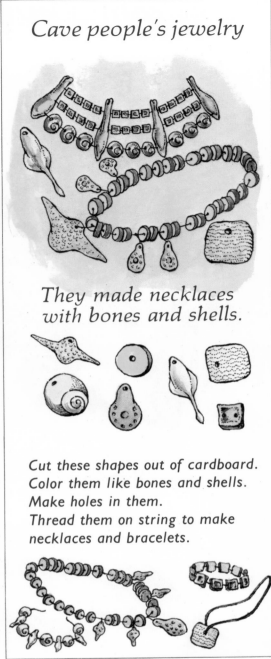

They made necklaces with bones and shells.

Cut these shapes out of cardboard.
Color them like bones and shells.
Make holes in them.
Thread them on string to make necklaces and bracelets.

How cave people made clothes

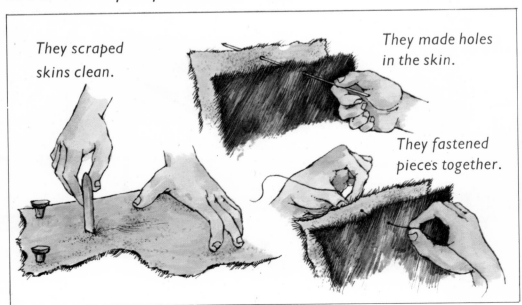

They scraped skins clean.

They made holes in the skin.

They fastened pieces together.

The pyramid builders of Egypt

In Egypt long, long ago they built huge pyramids.
They made the pyramids of stone. They buried
their kings and queens inside the pyramids.

They carved out great blocks
of stone.

They measured the blocks
and cut them to the right size.

They pulled the blocks
to the site of the pyramid.

*They carried the huge stone blocks
down the river on boats.*

*They pulled the blocks
up long earth ramps.*

*With the blocks of stone
they built the huge pyramids.*

13

The gods of Ancient Greece

Long ago people who lived in Greece
believed there were many gods.
They told stories about the gods.

Zeus
was the ruler
of all the gods.

Eros
was the god
of love.

Hermes
was the gods'
messenger.

Apollo
was the god
of music.

Poseidon
was the god
of the sea.

Athena
was the goddess
of wisdom
and weaving.

Demeter
was the goddess
of the harvest.

Here are some of the stories about the gods
and the ancient Greek people.

How trouble came to the world

The gods sent a box to Pandora
and her husband. The gods
told them not to open it.

Pandora wanted to see inside the box.
She opened it.
All the troubles of the world flew out.

How Arachne became a spider

Arachne wove a beautiful cloth.
She thought she could weave
better than the goddess Athena.

Athena had a
weaving match with Arachne.
Arachne was rude to Athena.

Athena changed
Arachne
into a spider.
"You shall spin and
weave forever!"
Athena said.

Prometheus steals fire

Prometheus stole fire from the gods.
He gave it to the people.

Zeus, the ruler of the gods,
was very, very angry.
First, he punished Prometheus.
He tied him to a rock for ever and ever.
Then, he sent a flood to the world.
The waters covered the whole world.

Life in Ancient Rome

The Romans were great builders.
They were great soldiers too.
They conquered many lands.

Romans built temples for their gods.

An aqueduct carries water.

A villa to live in.

a litter

a chariot

Romans built long straight roads.

A Roman book

Roman numbers

1	2	3	4	5	6	7	8	9	10
I	II	III	IV	V	VI	VII	VIII	IX	X

The Roman army

Some soldiers went on foot.
Some soldiers rode horses.

Roman soldiers
had swords and
javelins.
A javelin
is a light spear.

A centurion
led
100
soldiers.

The soldiers could protect themselves
with their shields like a tortoise.

Making a mosaic

You need:
colored paper
cardboard

scissors
glue

Cut the paper into scraps.

Romans decorated
their floors with
pictures made with
little bits of stone.
These pictures
are called mosaics.

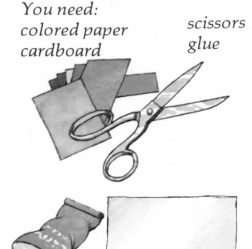

Stick the scraps on the cardboard to make a picture.

How people measured

This man is using
stones to count.
Each stone is one sheep.

The Chinese used a frame
of beads to count. It was
called an abacus.

The Incas tied knots
in rope to help them count.

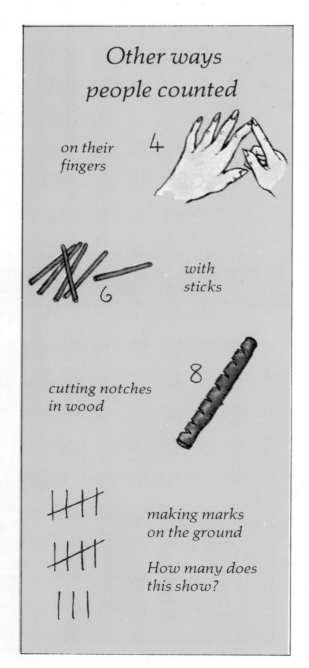

Other ways people counted

on their fingers   4

with sticks   6

cutting notches in wood   8

making marks on the ground

How many does this show?

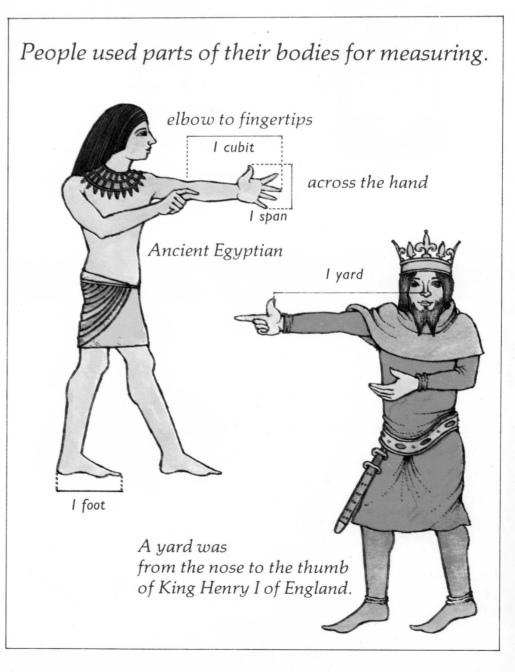

People used parts of their bodies for measuring.

elbow to fingertips

1 cubit

across the hand

1 span

Ancient Egyptian

1 foot

1 yard

A yard was
from the nose to the thumb
of King Henry I of England.

Measuring time

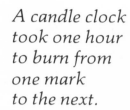

A candle clock took one hour to burn from one mark to the next.

A water clock empties to show the time.

The sun's shadow tells the time on a sundial.

The sand took one hour to drop through an hourglass.

Make a water clock

Take two paper cups.
Make a tiny hole near the bottom of one cup.

Put the cups like this in a bowl.
Fill the top cup with water.

Put a mark inside the cup at the water level.
Make a mark every quarter of an hour as the water goes down.
Fill the cup again.
Measure time with your water clock.

A sun clock

Put a long stick in the ground.
Mark where its shadow falls at different times.
Tomorrow, look at your sun clock to tell the time.

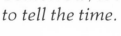

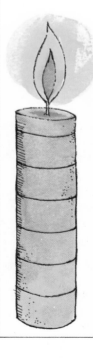

Make a candle clock

Mark lines around a candle. How long does it take to burn between each mark?

When Vikings roamed the seas

The Vikings
sailed across the sea
in their longboats.

A Viking settlement

building a hut

making clay pots   making metal weapons

They attacked
other countries.

Then they
settled in them.

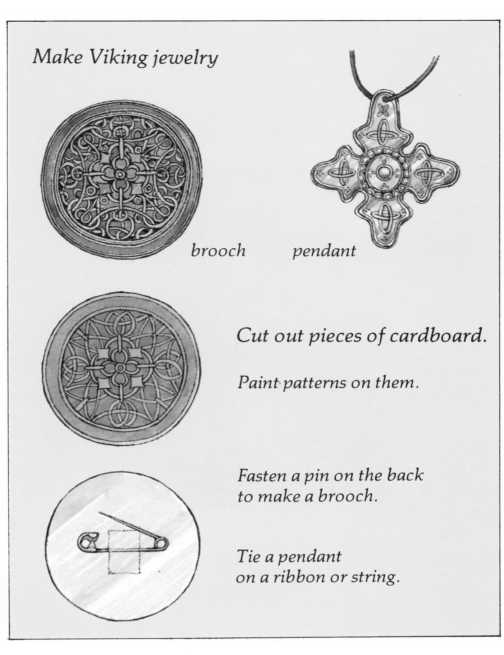

Make Viking jewelry

brooch　　pendant

Cut out pieces of cardboard.

Paint patterns on them.

Fasten a pin on the back
to make a brooch.

Tie a pendant
on a ribbon or string.

Everyone lived
together
in the
big house.

Long ago in China

The Chinese built a great wall around China to keep out their enemies.

The Chinese ships were called junks. They sailed to many lands.

The Chinese invented many things.

They invented fireworks.

They made kites.

They made painted china.

They made silk cloth. They painted pictures on silk.

The Chinese people wore beautiful clothes.

This is an actor.

child

silk robe

woman

fan

man

bow

helmet

soldier

sword

Chinese writing is difficult to read. It is written downward. The letters are painted with a brush.

Chinese people eat with chopsticks.

Find two straight sticks. Can you pick up your food with them?

People who lived in castles

lord   lady   children   steward   serving woman   knight   soldiers   servant

Long ago these people lived in a castle.
They lived there to be safe from their enemies.

Here is the castle they lived in.

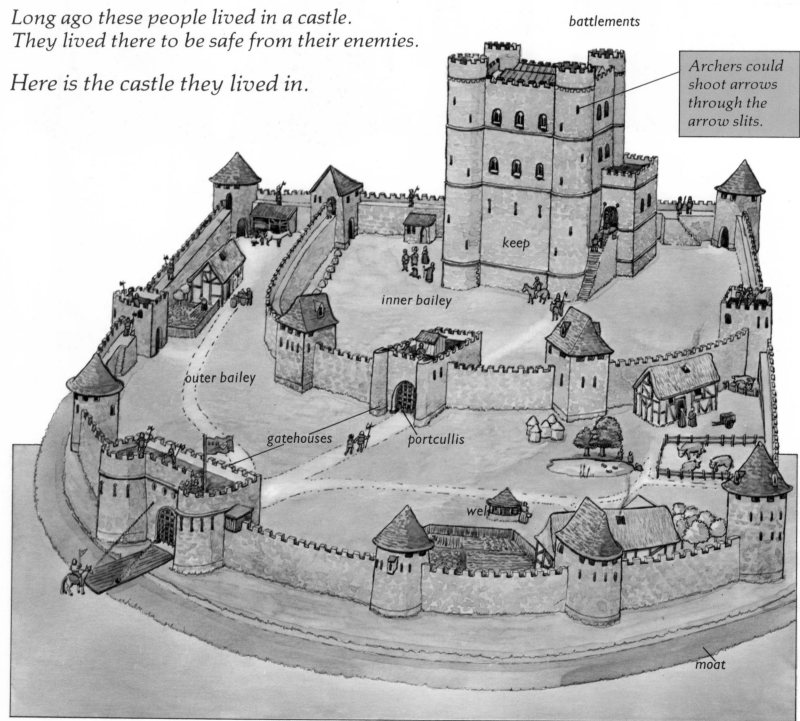

battlements

Archers could shoot arrows through the arrow slits.

keep

inner bailey

outer bailey

gatehouses   portcullis

well

moat

The lord and his family lived in the keep.

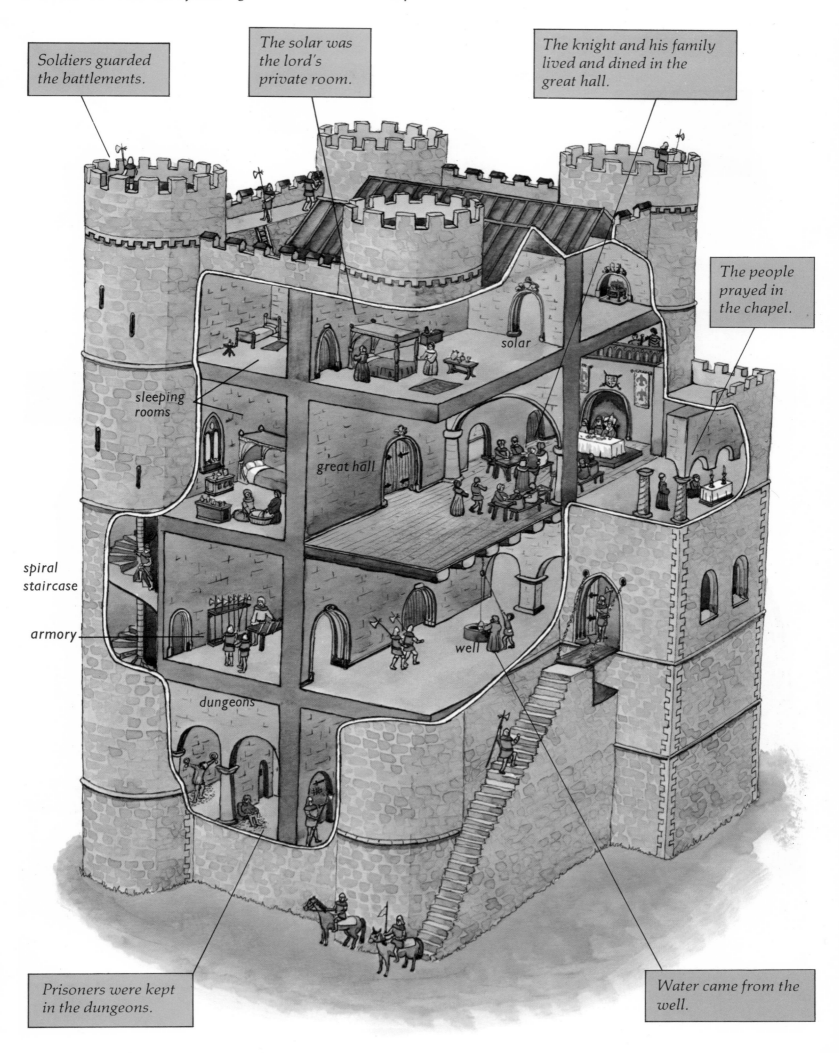

Soldiers guarded the battlements.

The solar was the lord's private room.

The knight and his family lived and dined in the great hall.

The people prayed in the chapel.

solar

sleeping rooms

great hall

spiral staircase

armory

well

dungeons

Prisoners were kept in the dungeons.

Water came from the well.

Knights in armor

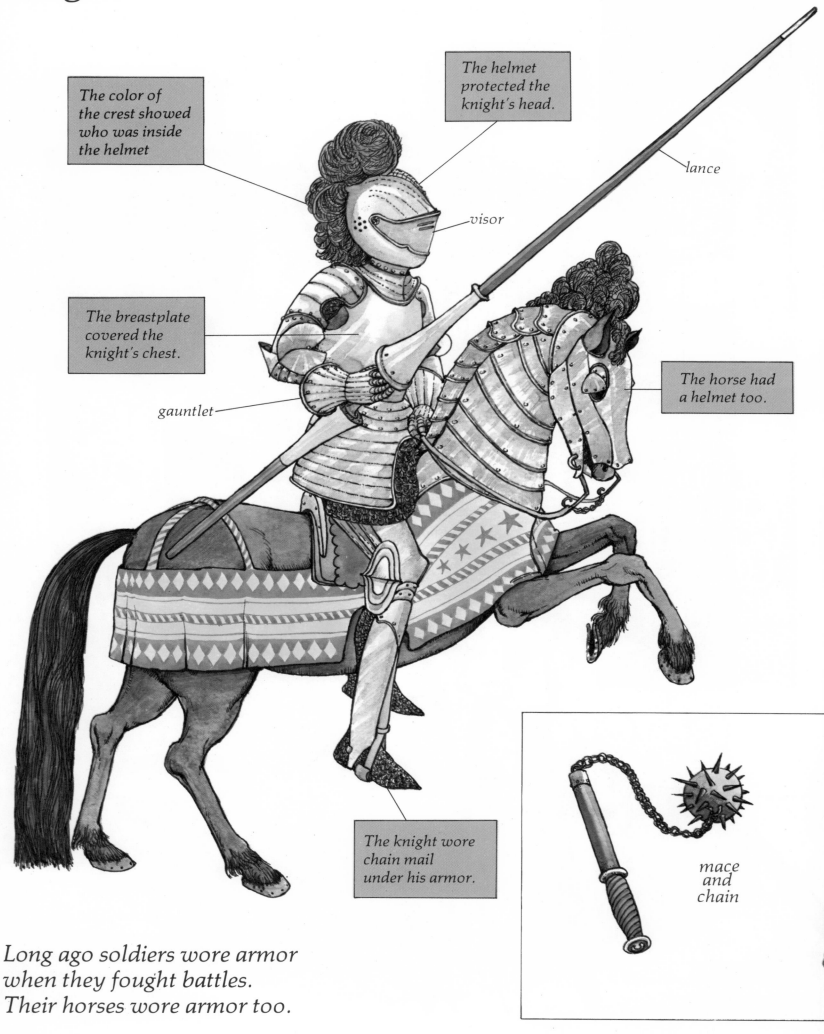

The color of the crest showed who was inside the helmet

The helmet protected the knight's head.

lance

visor

The breastplate covered the knight's chest.

gauntlet

The horse had a helmet too.

The knight wore chain mail under his armor.

mace and chain

Long ago soldiers wore armor when they fought battles. Their horses wore armor too.

A knight could raise the visor on his helmet.

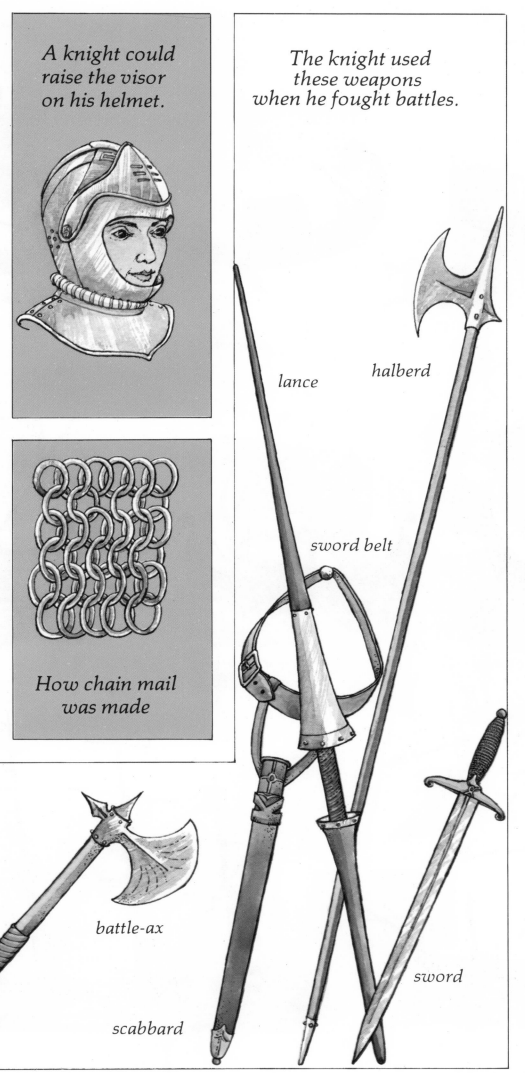

How chain mail was made

battle-ax

The knight used these weapons when he fought battles.

lance

halberd

sword belt

scabbard

sword

How to make a shield and sword

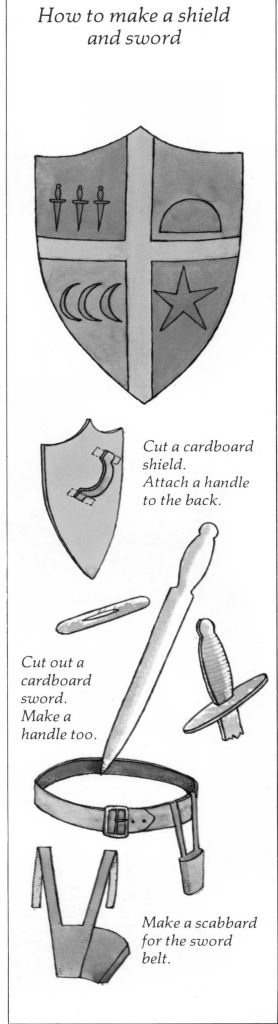

Cut a cardboard shield. Attach a handle to the back.

Cut out a cardboard sword. Make a handle too.

Make a scabbard for the sword belt.

Ships of long ago

People have paddled and sailed across water for thousands of years.

Cavemen paddled dugout canoes.

Coracles were made of skin.

This man has put a sail on his raft.

Egyptian river boats were made of reeds.

This Egyptian boat could go to sea.

The Romans steered this ship with an oar.

The Vikings crossed the oceans in their longboats.

East Indiamen carried cargo between Asia and Europe.

Clipper ships went very fast.

The Greeks had slaves to row their galleys.

Christopher Columbus discovered America in a ship like this.

Spanish galleons had three masts.

This ship used steam power to cross the Atlantic in 1838.

Use a walnut shell for the hull.

Put a bit of modeling clay inside it.

Cut out a paper sail. Attach it to a toothpick.

Stick the sail into the clay in the shell.

Sail your boat.

Try different shaped sails.

Inside a man-o-war

Sailing ships like this went
right around the world.
They were used to fight battles
at sea, too.
The sailors worked the sails with ropes.
They had to know what every bit
of rope did.

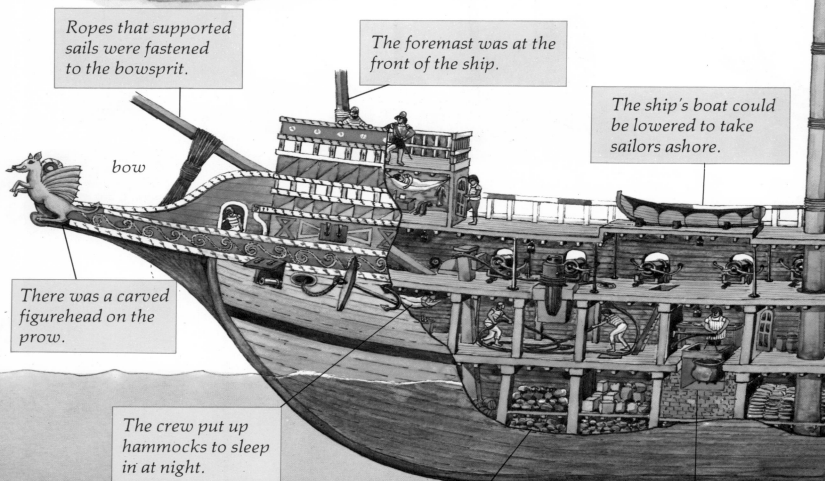

The mainmast was at the
center of the ship.

Ropes that supported
sails were fastened
to the bowsprit.

The foremast was at the
front of the ship.

The ship's boat could
be lowered to take
sailors ashore.

bow

There was a carved
figurehead on the
prow.

The crew put up
hammocks to sleep
in at night.

When there was not much
cargo they put stones
in the hold. This kept
the ship steady.

The food was cooked
in the galley.

foremast

mainmast

mizzenmast

maintopsail

fore-topsail

mizzen

foresail

mainsail

The lookout man could watch from the crow's-nest.

spritsail

bow

stern

The cannons fired through holes in the sides of the ship.

The mizzenmast was near the back of the ship.

The captain and officers stood on the poop deck. They told the sailors what to do.

stern

The captain had a comfortable cabin.

The rudder was moved by the whipstaff. When the rudder moved the ship turned.

keel

The cargo was stored in the holds.

Farming in the past

Long ago people had no machinery
to help them on their farms.

Oxen pulled the plow to dig the ground.

The farmer sowed
the seeds by hand.

The farmer cut the wheat with a sickle.

Farming today

A tractor
pulls the
plow.

A tractor pulls
the seeder.

The farmer took the wheat on a wagon
to the windmill.
The windmill ground the grain to make flour.

When all the wheat was harvested, there was a party.

A combine harvester
cuts the wheat.

A tractor carries
the straw.

Food from long ago

People used to eat all sorts of strange food.

Knights in castles ate whole baby pigs, roast swans and stuffed peacocks.

A whole ox would be roasted on a spit over the fire.

People eat all these things!

snails   frogs' legs   octopus   snakes

Christmas pudding

The pudding mixture was tied in a cloth and cooked.

The pudding came out round.

Pemmican

Hunters dried meat over a fire so it would last on their long journeys.

They made it into cakes. It was called pemmican.

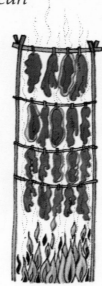

lobsters   crabs

People used to have much bigger meals long ago.

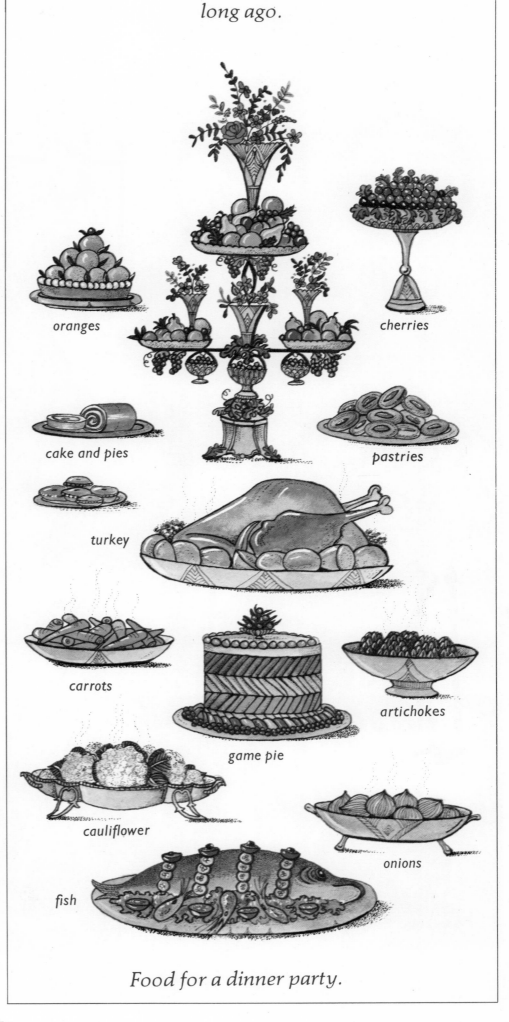

oranges

cherries

cake and pies

pastries

turkey

carrots

artichokes

game pie

cauliflower

onions

fish

Food for a dinner party.

How people lived in palaces

King Louis the fourteenth of France built himself a great palace at Versailles.

The King   The Queen

A day in the life of the King

When the King wakes, the noblemen help him to dress.

In the morning, the King goes hunting in the forest.

In the afternoon, the King walks in his garden.

In the evening, there is a banquet.

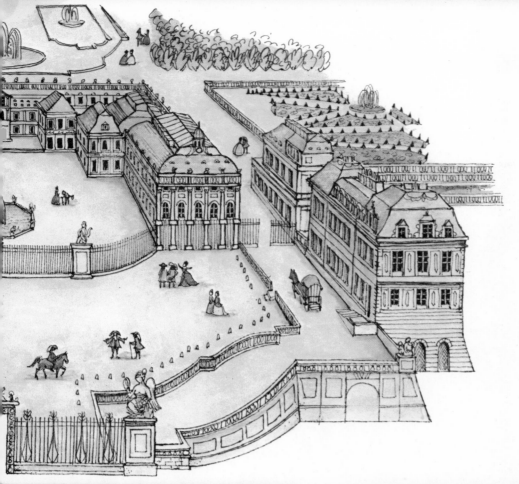

People come to see the King.
They ask him to help them.

After the banquet, the King and his courtiers
go to a masked ball.

The American Indians

Long, long ago only American Indians lived
in North America.
There were many different tribes of Indians.
Here is a camp of a tribe of Indians
who lived on the Great Plains.

These Indians lived
in tepees.

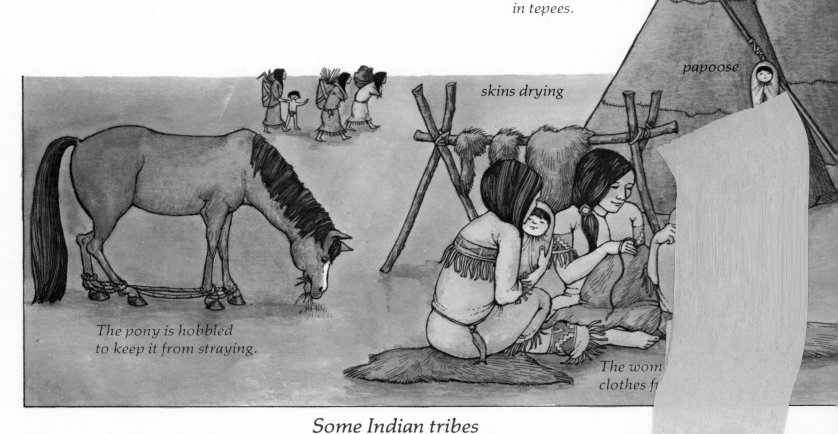

skins drying

papoose

The pony is hobbled
to keep it from straying.

The wom
clothes f

Some Indian tribes

Navaho

Iroquois

Sioux

Apache

The
Haida
people
built
totem
poles.

sending smoke signals

hunting buffalo

The soldiers and hunters were called braves.

The Chief in his feather headdress.

Sign language

When one tribe spoke to another tribe, they used sign language.

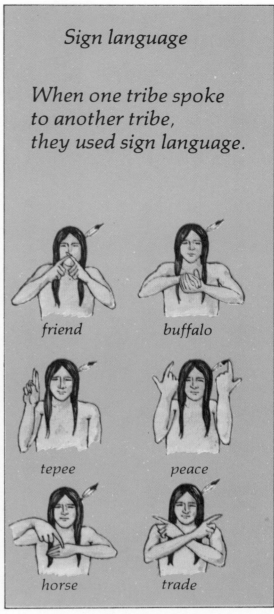

friend buffalo

tepee peace

horse trade

Making a headdress

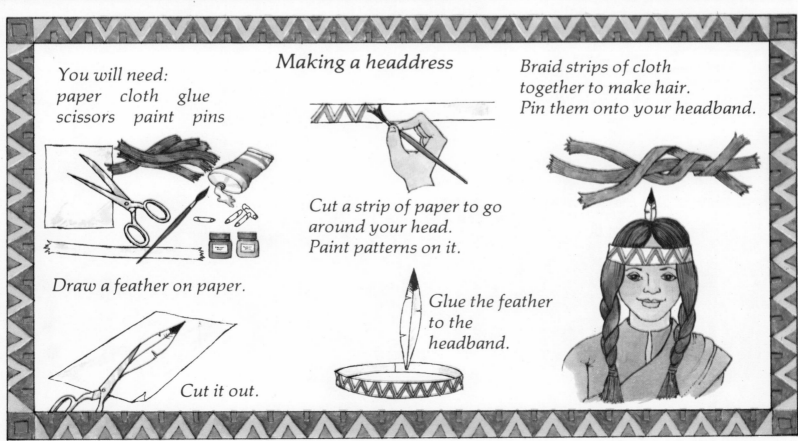

You will need:
paper cloth glue
scissors paint pins

Draw a feather on paper.

Cut it out.

Cut a strip of paper to go around your head. Paint patterns on it.

Glue the feather to the headband.

Braid strips of cloth together to make hair. Pin them onto your headband.

Settlers and Pioneers

Long ago people left Europe.
They came to live in America.
They were looking for a better way of life.

They had to work very hard.
They cleared land to make
their farms.
They built houses with logs.
Can you see the woman
making candles?

Inside a cabin

spinning wool

cleaning a gun

Going west

The settlers discovered these things in America.

potatoes

tobacco

turkeys

corn

tomatoes

More and more people came to live in America.
They were looking for rich farm land.
Sometimes they traveled right across America.
They carried everything with them in wagons.
Sometimes the Indians tried to stop them.

The days of the cowboys

Cowboys looked after cattle on the wide open plains of the West.
The cowboy's horse was very important to him. It took him everywhere.

The cowboy catches cattle with his long rope or lasso.

The big stetson keeps the sun off.

Gloves protect his hands.

Chaps protect his legs.

He has a big saddle.

Back at the ranch

The cowboys live in the bunkhouse.

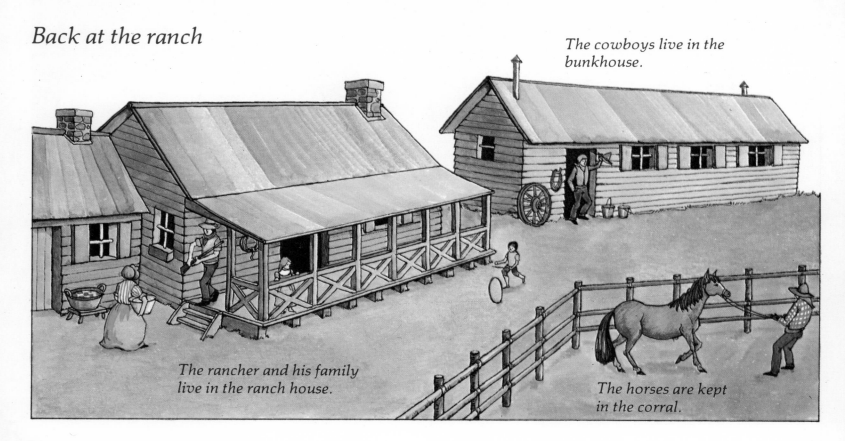

The rancher and his family live in the ranch house.

The horses are kept in the corral.

Out on the range

The cattle roamed wild on the prairies.
Each ranch marked its own cattle with a brand or mark.

This cowboy is catching a calf
with his lasso.

The brand is burned onto the calf
with a branding iron.

Here are
some brands.

Rocking A   Swinging M   Lazy 8   Star R

The cowboys rounded up the cattle
to take them to market.

The chuck wagon
carries the
cowboys'
food and water.

Machines long ago

We have a lot of machines in our homes.

When these machines were invented.
they looked very different.

Here are some of them.

This woman is
using a
vacuum cleaner.

This woman has to scrub
the floor.

This washing machine was turned with a
handle. The water was wrung out of
the clothes with a mangle.

How things
have changed

The first tea-maker:
When the alarm
went, a match lit
a lamp.
When the water
boiled, the kettle
tipped
the water into
a teapot.

1902

Today

44

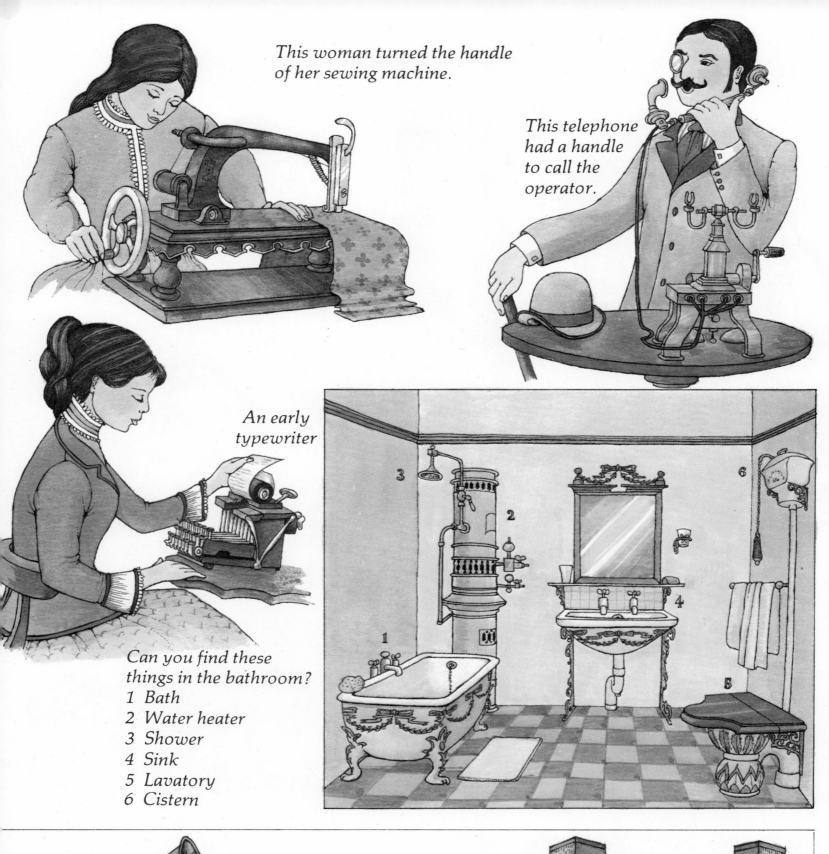

This woman turned the handle of her sewing machine.

This telephone had a handle to call the operator.

An early typewriter

Can you find these things in the bathroom?
1 Bath
2 Water heater
3 Shower
4 Sink
5 Lavatory
6 Cistern

This gramophone or record player had to be wound up with a handle.

1900

Today

About children

Stone Age   Ancient Egypt   Ancient Rome

Babies

American Indians carried their babies or papooses on their backs.

This baby is in a wooden rocking cradle.

Babies were dressed in lots of clothes like their mothers.

France in 1066

Italy in 1400

Spain in 1600

Holland in 1700

France in 1750

England in 1800

the USA in 1850

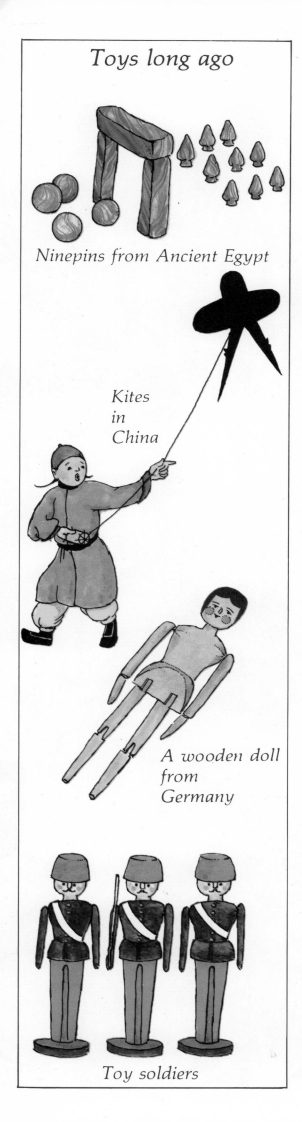

Toys long ago

Ninepins from Ancient Egypt

Kites in China

A wooden doll from Germany

Toy soldiers

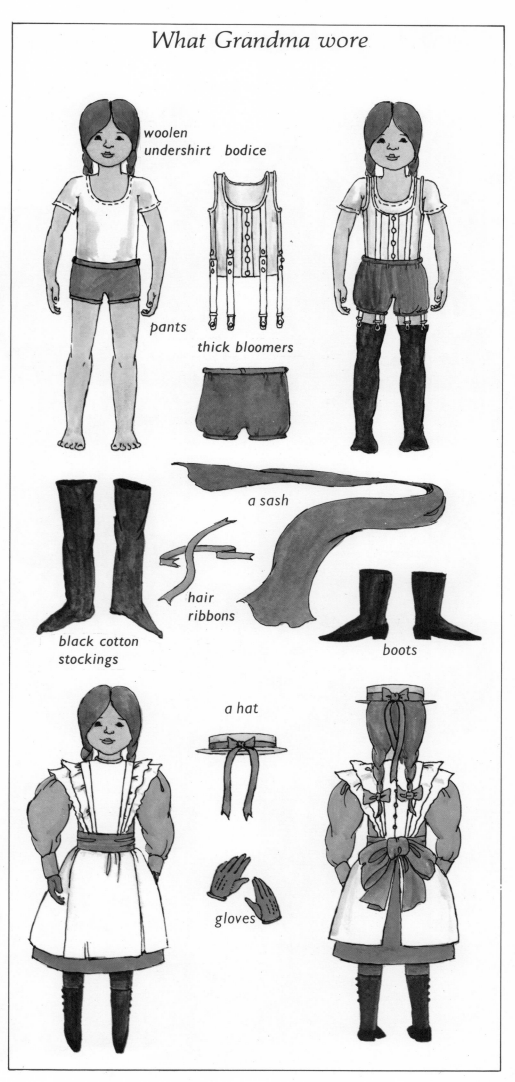

What Grandma wore

woolen undershirt   bodice

pants

thick bloomers

a sash

hair ribbons

black cotton stockings

boots

a hat

gloves

The story of transport

Cave men had to walk.   Later people tamed horses.   An ox pulled a cart with wheels.

A mail coach
1830

A hobby horse
bicycle
1817

A steam road carriage
1858

Model T Ford
1908

Sports car
1970

Citroen 1938

Stephenson's Rocket 1829

A royal carriage.

The Benz car had a gasoline engine. 1899

A train in 1900

Engine 1935

Electric locomotive

A Japanese monorail train

Pulling a load on rollers is easier than pulling it on the ground.

Wheels make it even easier.

A pulley helps to lift things.

Wheels can turn other wheels.

Gear wheels work the inside of a clock.

Car wheels have tires.

Grooved wheels hold trains on a track.

Early trains

First class passengers traveled inside.

Other passengers traveled in open cars.

Trains carry people and animals and all sorts of freight.

freight car

Trains like this carried people across the United States.

fireman engineer

The luggage went
in the luggage car.

The tender carried
coal for the engine.

Engines used steam
to drive them along the track.

passenger car sleeper mail car caboose

coal car cattle car tender engine

Along the roads

The first car
was like a carriage.
But it had a motor
instead of a horse.

bus 1912

fire engine 1913

Daimler 1886

Cars of yesterday and today

Gobron-Brillé 1904

Delage Runabout 1913

Mercedes 300 SL 1955
This car was known as
the Gull Wing.

Austin 7 1922

Cars at work

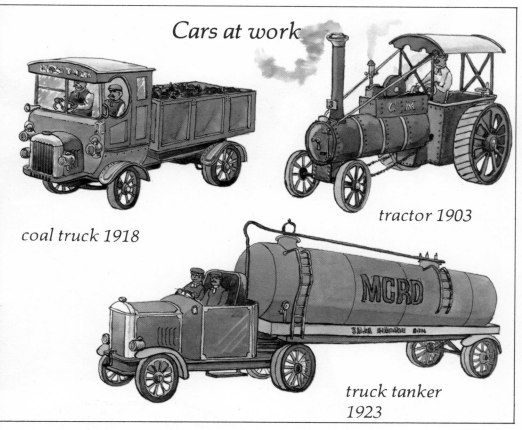

coal truck 1918

tractor 1903

truck tanker 1923

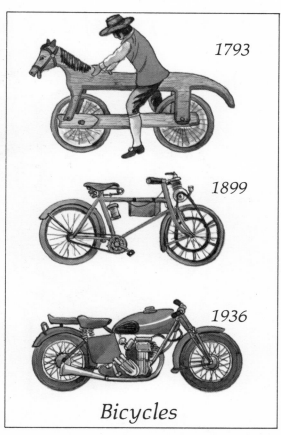

1793

1899

1936

Bicycles

Rolls Royce Phantom I 1925

Lotus Elan 1965

Powerful cars from many countries compete in motor races.

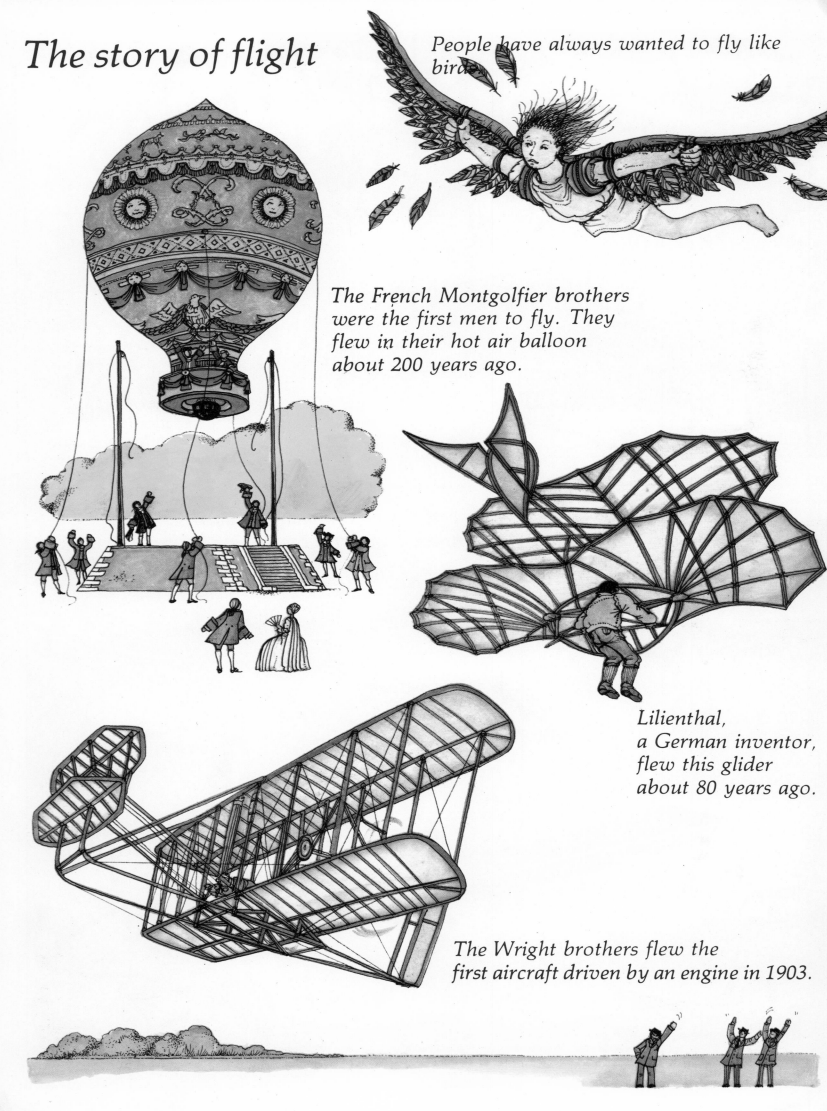

The story of flight

People have always wanted to fly like birds.

The French Montgolfier brothers were the first men to fly. They flew in their hot air balloon about 200 years ago.

Lilienthal, a German inventor, flew this glider about 80 years ago.

The Wright brothers flew the first aircraft driven by an engine in 1903.

Bleriot, a French pilot, flew across the sea from France to England in 1909.

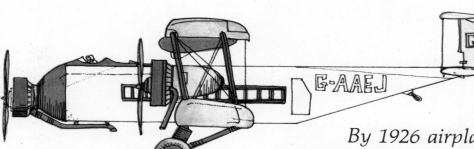

By 1926 airplanes were taking people all over the world.

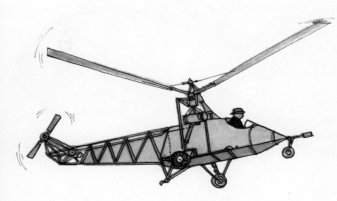

The first helicopter was flown in 1940.

Huge jet planes carry hundreds of people around the world.

How to make a paper glider

Fold a piece of paper in half.

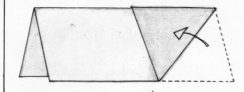

Fold the ends up on both sides.

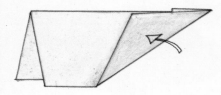

Fold both sides up again.

Fold the sides up for a third time.

Turn the glider over and it is ready to fly.

An old house in town

bedroom

bedroom

drawing room

dining room

hansom cab

attic

servant's bedroom

linen cupboard

bathroom

landing

billiard room

hall

maid

cook

kitchen

organ grinder

57

How a village grew

Long, long ago some people built a village near a river. They got their water from the river.

More people came to the village. They built a bridge across the river.

Railroads were invented. The trains brought more people and the town grew.

There were more factories, more bridges and more houses.

One family was rich. They built a big house.

The rich family built a factory. People came to work in it. They built more houses. The village was now a town.

The big house was torn down and a factory built.

Old houses were torn down. Tall new apartment buildings were built. Today the town is a big town.

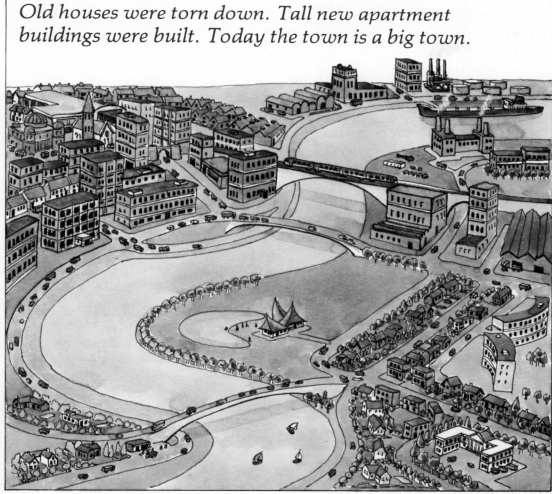

It's fun finding out

What are these? If you do not know, the numbers tell you which page to look at.

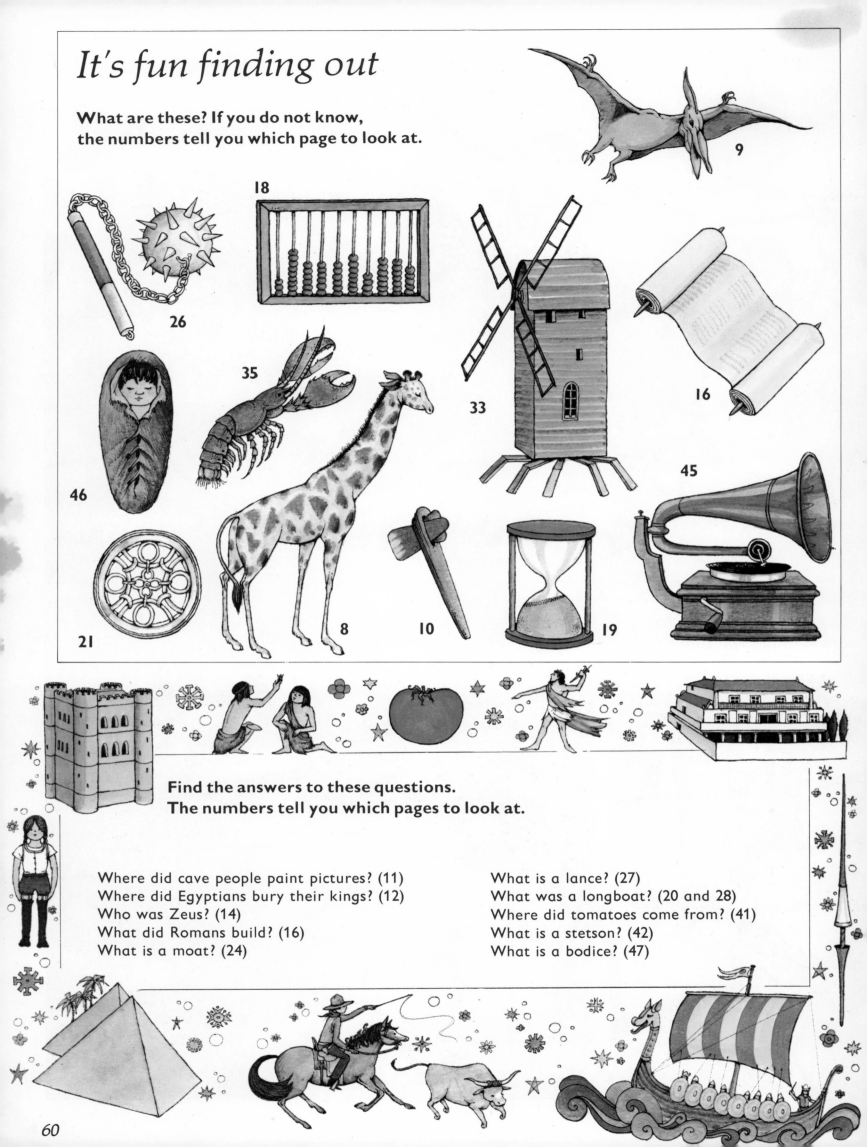

9

18

26

35

33

16

46

45

21

8

10

19

**Find the answers to these questions.
The numbers tell you which pages to look at.**

Where did cave people paint pictures? (11)
Where did Egyptians bury their kings? (12)
Who was Zeus? (14)
What did Romans build? (16)
What is a moat? (24)

What is a lance? (27)
What was a longboat? (20 and 28)
Where did tomatoes come from? (41)
What is a stetson? (42)
What is a bodice? (47)

Which one does not belong?

1

a
b
c
d

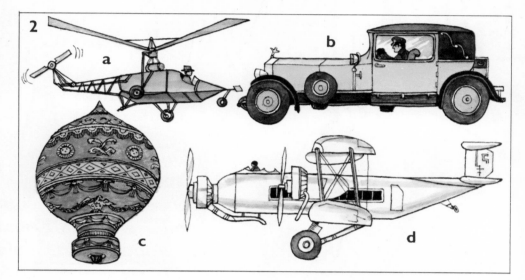

2

a
b
c
d

Who are these people?
The numbers tell you which page to look at.

38
14
16
26
12
40
10

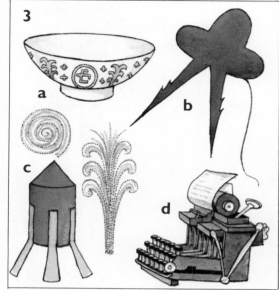

3

a
b
c
d

Answers

What are these?
8 giraffe
9 pteranodon
10 stone ax
16 Roman book
18 abacus
19 hourglass
21 Viking brooch
26 mace and chain
33 windmill
35 lobster
45 gramophone
46 papoose

These do not belong:
1 c The elephant is not a dinosaur.
2 b The car does not fly.
3 d The typewriter was not invented in ancient China.

Who are these people?
10 cave woman
12 Ancient Egyptian
14 Athena, a Greek god
16 Roman soldier
26 knight in armor
38 American Indian
40 Settler

Viking

shield

American Indian woman

abacus

bonnet

pyramid

turkey

cowboy

These are the pairs:

longboat and Viking
shield and knight
papoose and Indian woma
Diplodocus and Stegosauri
abacus and Chinese woma
Benz car and driver

Egyptian

stone ax

Roman book

girl

feathered hat

driver